A Home for Curly

Tony Mitton

Illustrated by Jo Brooker

Photographed by Keith Lillis

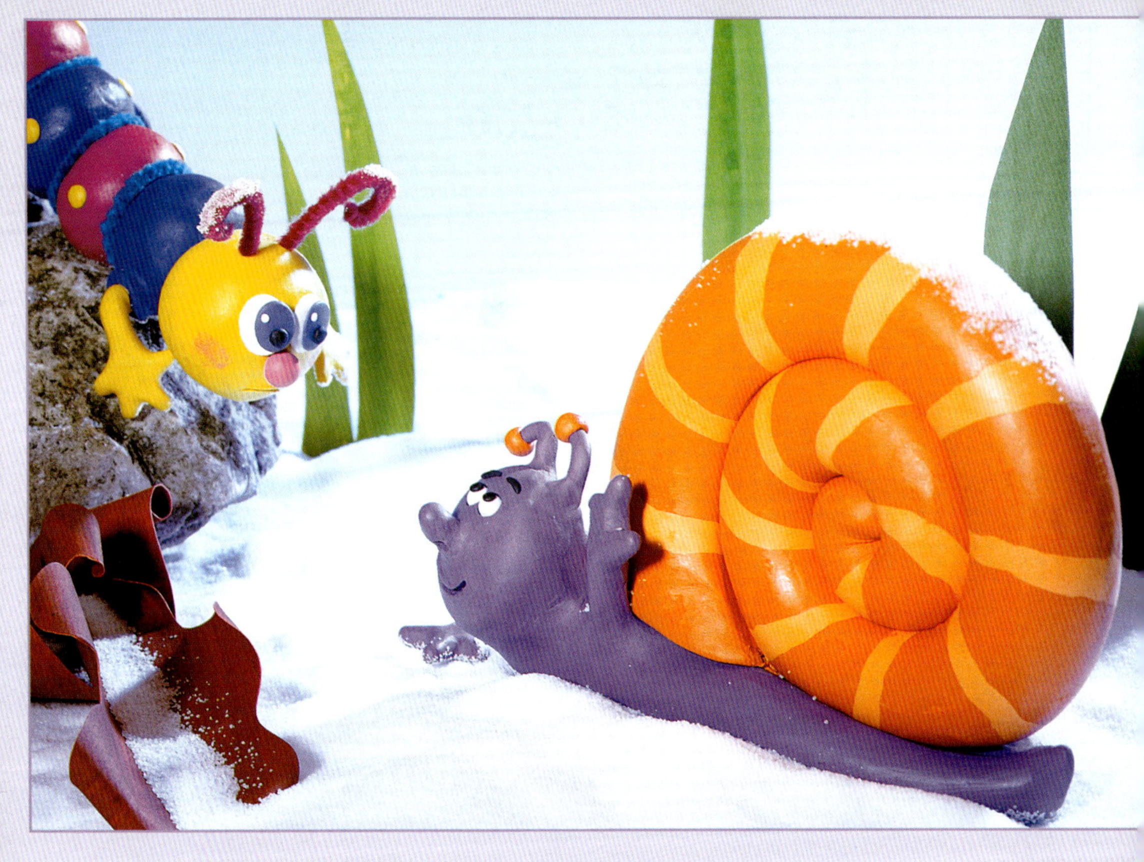

My home is a shell.

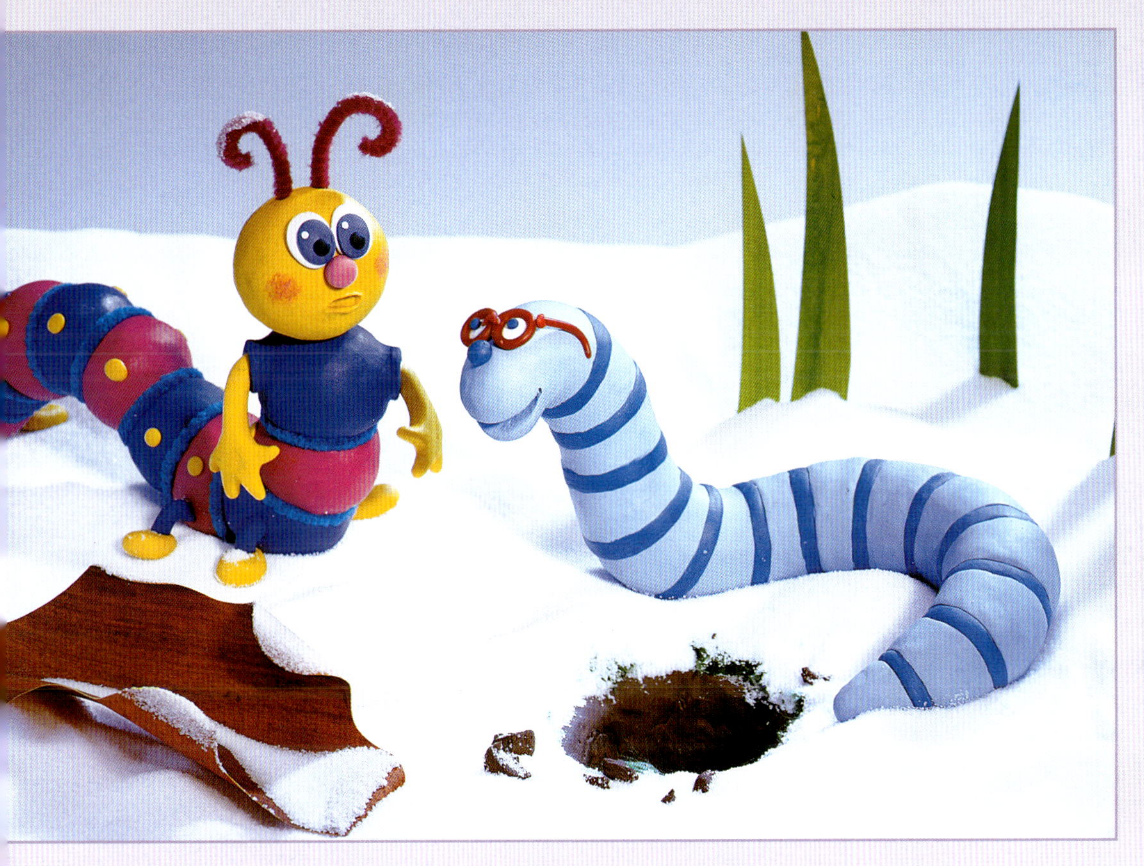

My home is a hole.

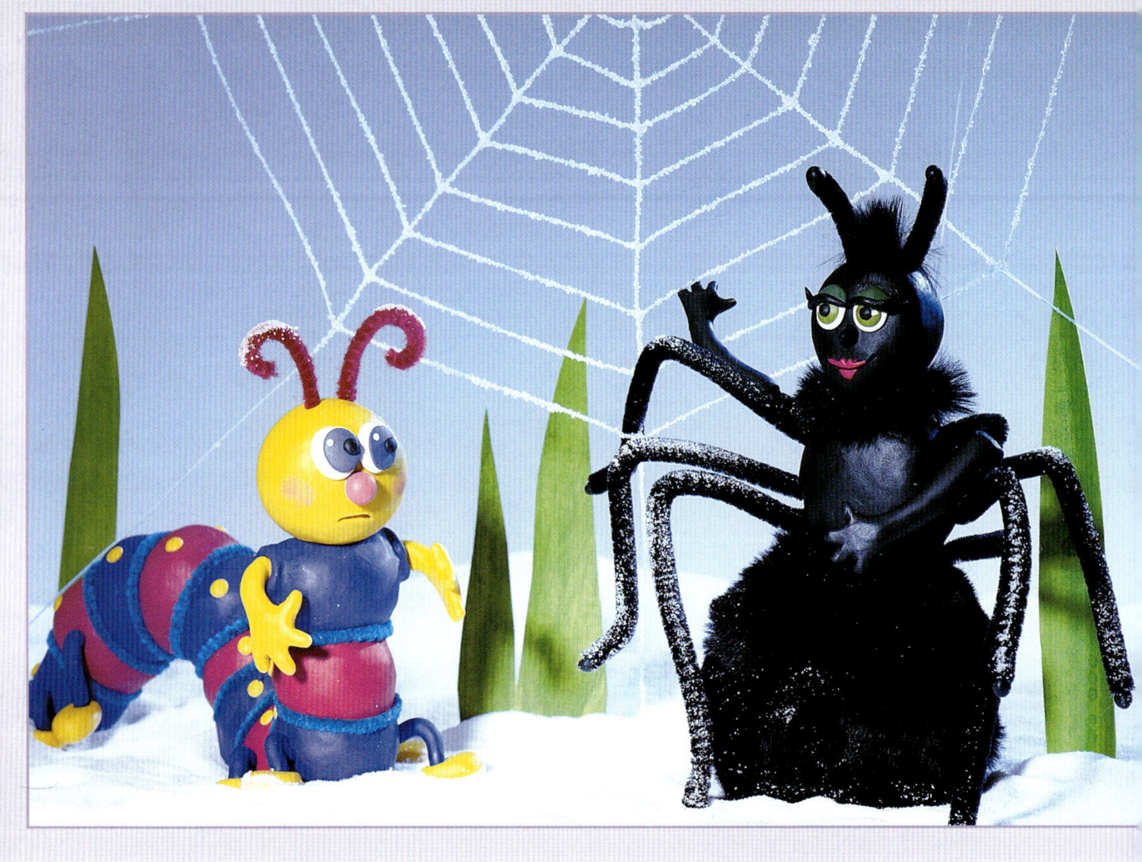

My home is a web.

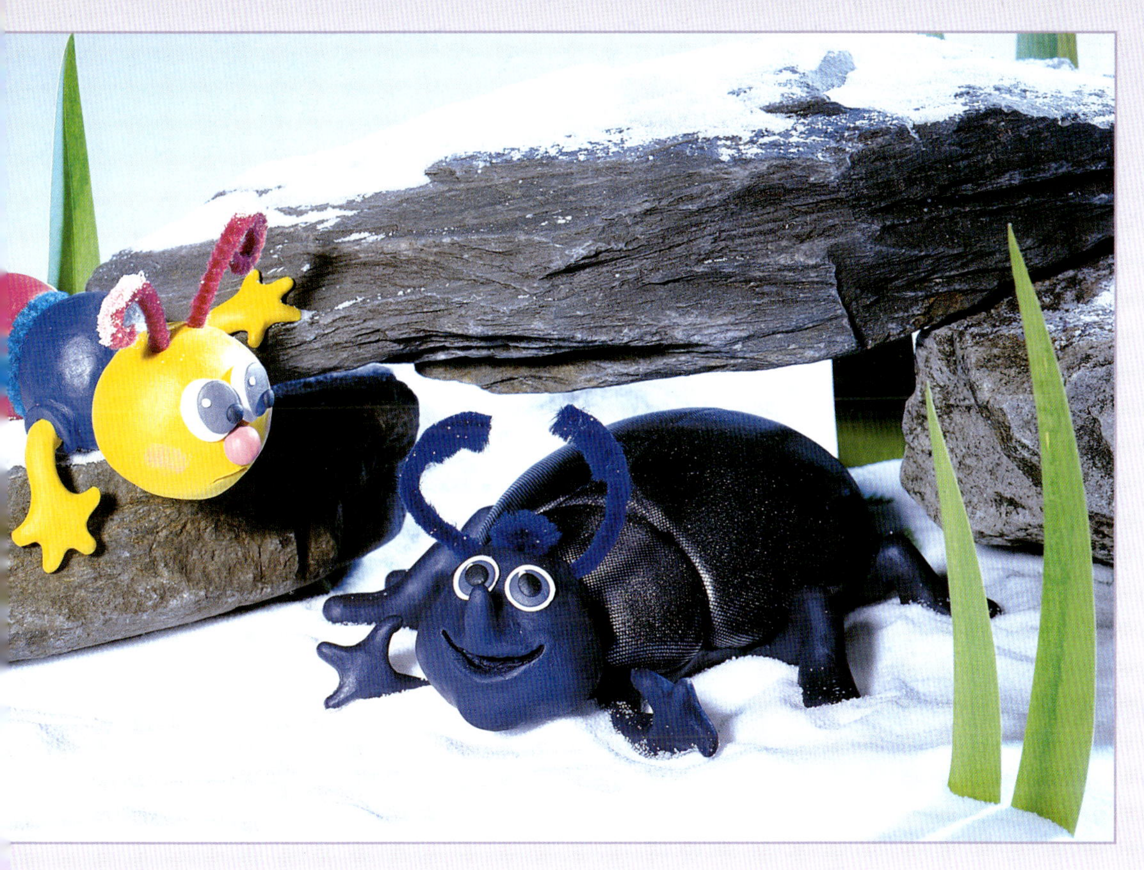

My home is a stone.

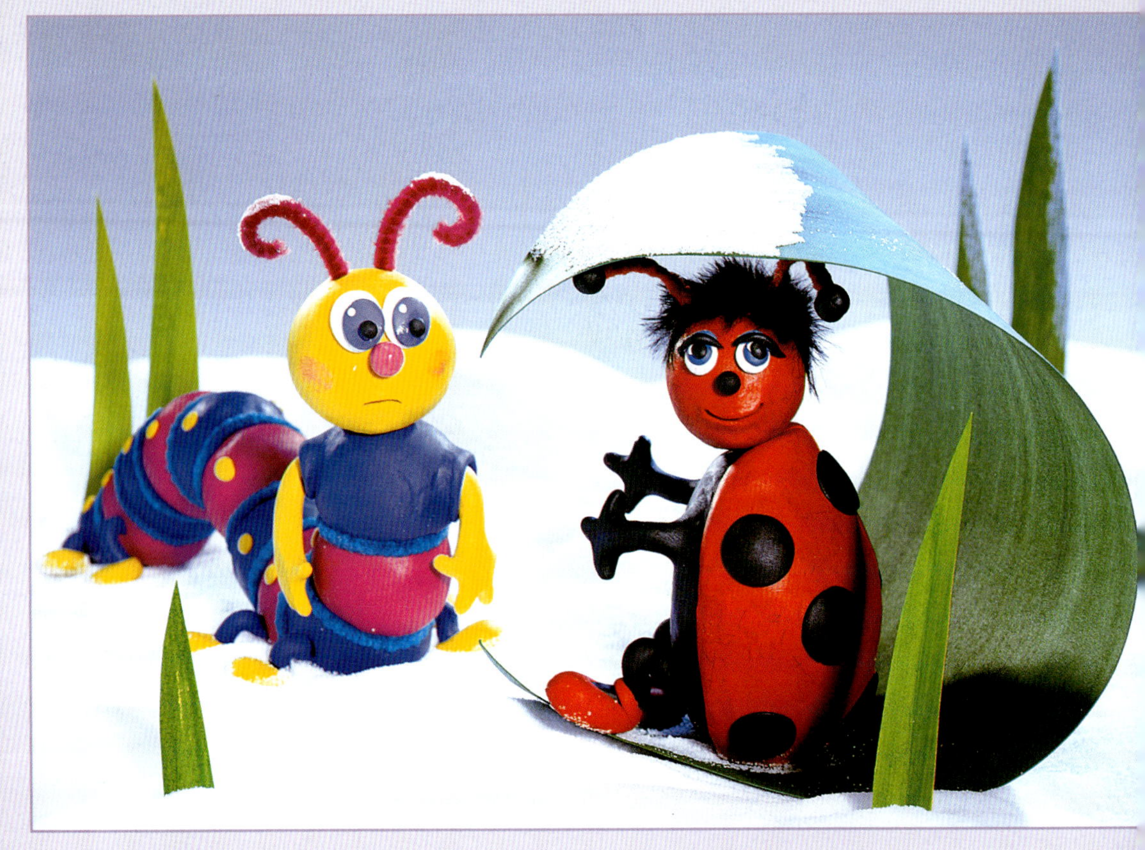

My home is a leaf.

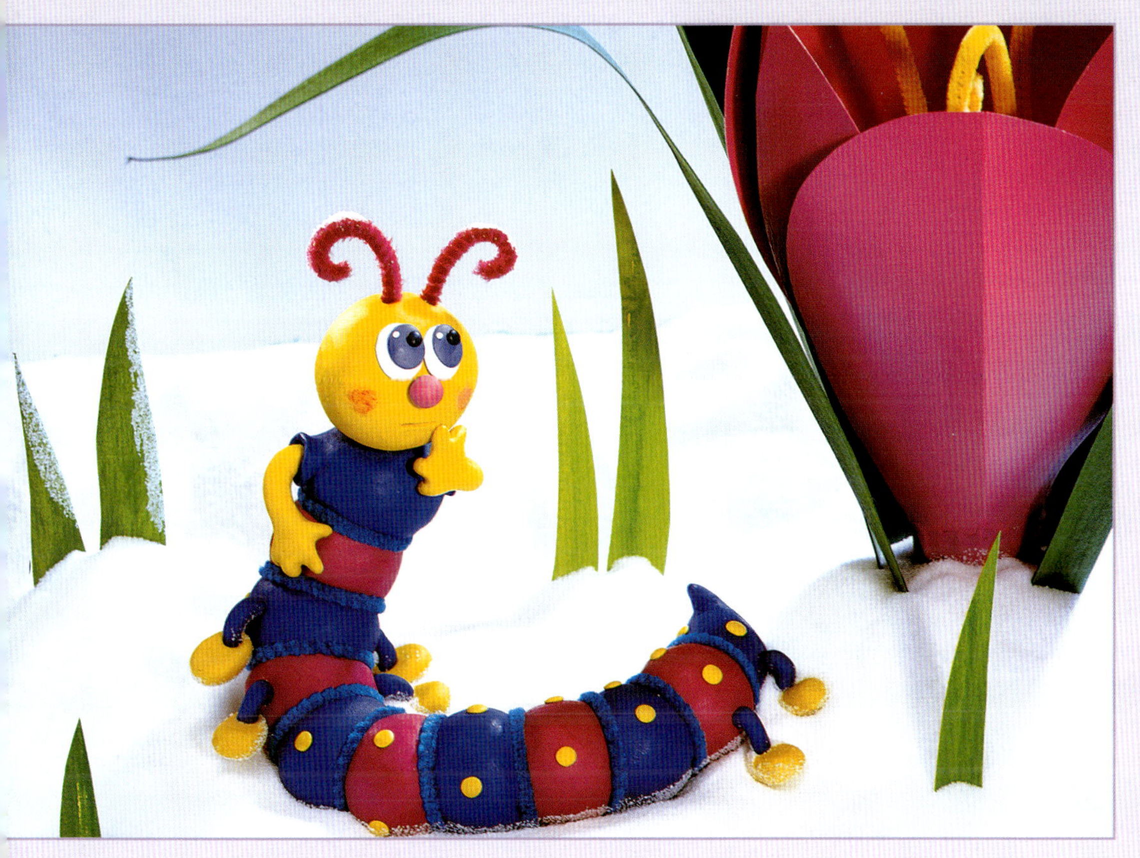

My home is . . .

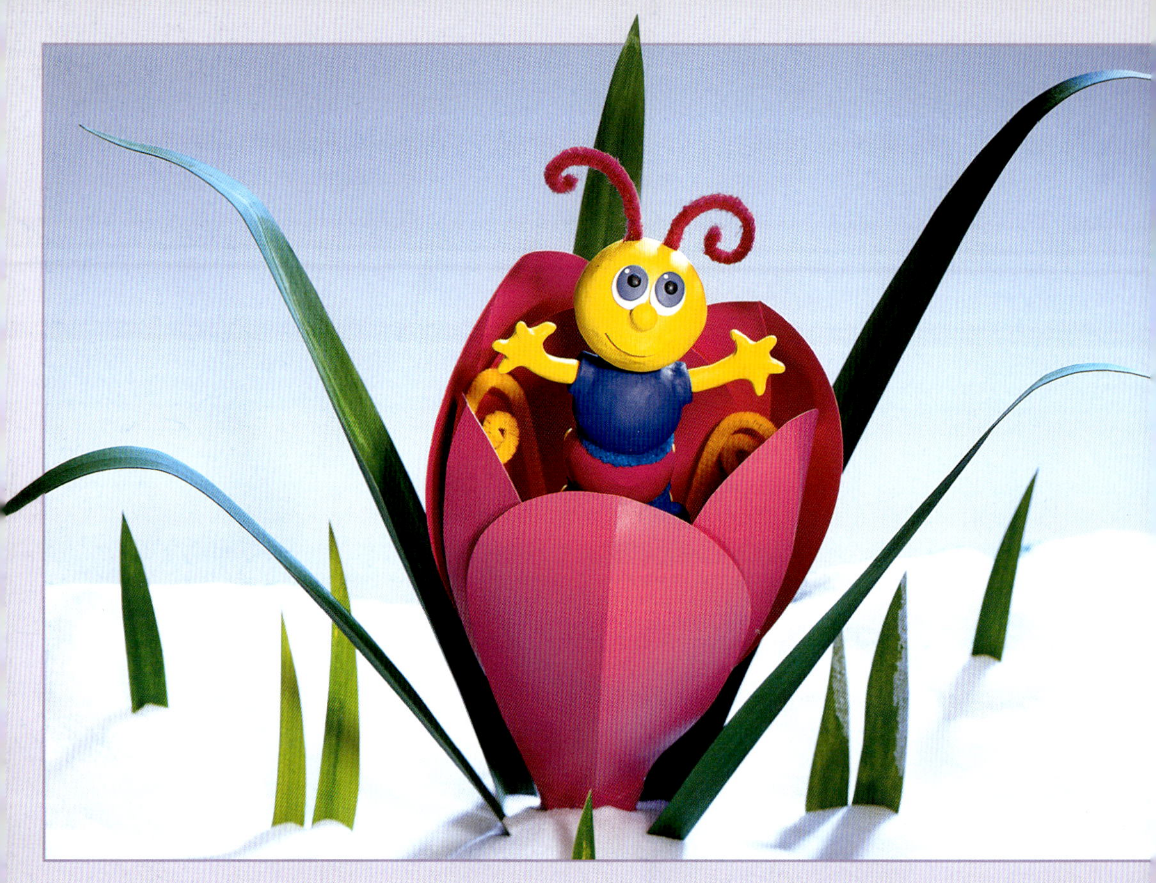

a flower!